J
Roy
Royston, Angela.
THE ELEPHANT .

ANIMAL LIFE STORIES

THE ELEPHANT

Published in 1989 by Warwick Press,
387 Park Avenue South, New York, N.Y. 10016.
First published in this edition by
Kingfisher Books, 1989. Some of the illustrations
in this book are taken from the First Look
at Nature series.

6 5 4 3 2 1

Printed in Spain

Library of Congress Catalog Card No. 89-50004
ISBN 0-531-19057-9

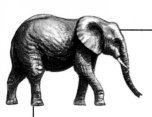
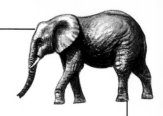

ANIMAL LIFE STORIES

THE ELEPHANT

Warwick Press
New York/London/Toronto/Sydney
1989

The mother elephant trudges over the hot dusty plains with her two calves. It has not rained now for nearly three months. All the elephants in the herd are thirsty, and their skin is dry and itchy. The mother elephant can smell water nearby although she cannot see it. She plods off to find it and the herd follows her.

Soon they reach a water hole. Zebras and gazelles are there already; but when they hear the heavy tread of the elephants, they run off to wait until the elephants have drunk their fill.

The leader of the herd drinks first, then the mother
elephant. She lies down and sucks the cool water
into her trunk, then sprays her back. Her bull calf
plunges right into the pool, squealing with delight.
His younger four-year-old sister splashes in after
him. They play together, wallowing in the mud and
squirting each other with water.

Three weeks later the elephants are still waiting for the rains to come. The grass is dry and there is little food. They knock over trees to reach the highest leaves and rip the bark off the baobab trees.

At last huge rain clouds begin to gather. An elephant sniffs the air and trumpets loudly as the first drops of rain fall. Soon the dry water holes and river beds will be full of water again.

For four weeks it has rained every day, and the land is green with new grass. As the elephant family wanders over the plains, two bull elephants follow them. The two elephants often wrestle together, pushing each other with their trunks to see which of them is the stronger.

One evening the stronger bull elephant lumbers over to the mother. He comes close to her and they touch each other with their trunks. He knows she is ready to mate now. When they have mated the bull elephant wanders off, and the mother goes back to join up with the herd.

11

Two months later the rains stop suddenly. As the sun scorches the land again, the elephants try to find shelter under the trees. Brilliant white egrets follow the elephants and eat the insects that bother them.

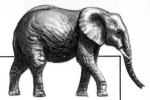

The elephant takes her calves to a water hole she knows. It has dried up but she can smell water under the surface. She digs a hole with her tusks. As the calves watch, it slowly fills up with water.

The seasons pass. For nearly two years a new calf grows inside the mother. When it is time for the calf to be born, she plods away to a secret place with two older females to help her. As soon as he is born, the new calf tries to stand up, but his knees are wobbly.

He flops to the ground. The big elephants nudge him with their trunks and tusks. They push him up again and again until he is strong enough to stand and suck his mother's milk. Two days later he is able to totter along with the herd as they move on.

The baby elephant is four months old now. One day he is grazing on his own when a hungry lioness creeps silently toward him. The egrets sense danger. They fly up in alarm and the mother elephant turns around.

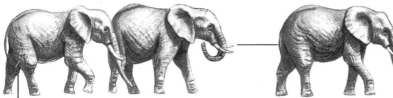

She trumpets fiercely and the lioness snarls. The elephant lowers her head and charges. Afraid of her tusks, the lioness backs off and moves away. After this the baby elephant keeps very close to his mother for safety.

The baby elephant grows bigger and stronger. He likes to play with the other young elephants, but his mother keeps him away from his rough older brother. One day his brother charges at his sister.

She gets a bad cut and one of her tusks is broken. The young bull is thirteen years old now, and it is time for him to leave the herd. The older cow elephants bang into him and push him away.

He squeals to his mother for help, but she ignores him. The young bull elephant watches as his family walks away, but he is not on his own for long. He joins a small herd of other bull elephants.

The female calf stays with the herd. She helps to look after the baby, making sure he is not left behind. In another five or six years she will be old enough to have a calf of her own.

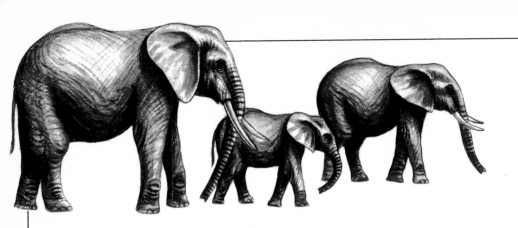

More about Elephants

Elephants are the largest living land animals. If one came into your living room, its head would probably touch the ceiling. They spend most of their day eating huge amounts of plants to feed their vast bodies.

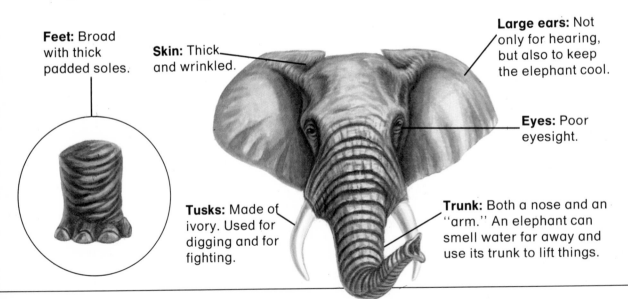

Feet: Broad with thick padded soles.

Skin: Thick and wrinkled.

Large ears: Not only for hearing, but also to keep the elephant cool.

Eyes: Poor eyesight.

Tusks: Made of ivory. Used for digging and for fighting.

Trunk: Both a nose and an "arm." An elephant can smell water far away and use its trunk to lift things.

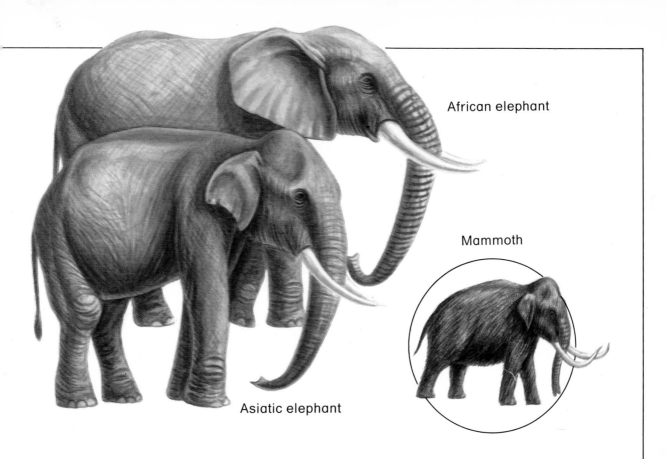

African elephant

Mammoth

Asiatic elephant

The elephant in this story is an African elephant. It is the largest of its kind and lives in central and southern Africa. The only other elephants are the Asiatic elephants which live in the jungles of India and Southeast Asia. A very long time ago, elephants called mammoths lived in the colder lands of Europe and Asia. They had long hair and huge curving tusks.

Some Special Words

Baobab tree These have a woody pulp inside. When plants and water are scarce, elephants rip off the bark and chew the pulp.

Bull Male elephant.

Calf Young elephant.

Cow Female elephant.

Egrets White wading birds. They eat the insects that bother elephants. When danger comes the egrets fly up in a panic.

Gazelle A kind of small deer.

Rains In central Africa spring, summer, fall, and winter are not very different from each other. Instead, the year is divided into dry periods when there is no rain and rainy seasons when there is heavy rain at some time every day.

Water hole A pool or lake where animals come to drink. In the dry season water holes often dry up.